IN AN EMERGENCY

Call the
Fire and Rescue
Service

Cath Senker

Photography by Howard Davies

W

First published in 2010 by
Franklin Watts
338 Euston Road
London NW1 3BH

Franklin Watts Australia
Level 17/207 Kent Street
Sydney NSW 2000

Series editor: Julia Bird

Design: Nimbus Design

Photography: Howard Davies

A CIP catalogue record for this book is available from the British Library.

ISBN 978 0 7496 9572 9

Dewey classification: 363.3'7

Printed in China

Franklin Watts is a division of Hachette Children's Books, an Hachette UK company.
www.hachette.co.uk

Acknowledgements

The author and photographer would like to thank the following for their help in the production of this book: East Sussex Fire and Rescue Service: staff and trainees at Maresfield Training Centre; Zoe Bowman and Blue Watch at Preston Circus fire station, Brighton; the staff at Eastbourne control centre; Allison Gilson; Steve Wright. West Sussex Fire and Rescue Service: Abigail Link and the VCS team at Shoreham Fire Station; Gary Towson. We would also to thank Alexa de Castilho and Loli Castilho Mills; Phaedra and Nestor Middleton; David, Avni, Bela and Luke Thomas; Finley Walsh.

Picture acknowledgements

East Sussex Fire & Rescue Service: 20 (Nick Tapsell), 21, 24; London Fire Brigade 22, 23. All other photographs by Howard Davies.

The photographs in this book feature firefighters and civilian models.

Cover picture: Trainee firefighters learn to use water hoses.

614.843

Contents

Words in **bold** can be found in the glossary on page 28.

The fire and rescue team

The fire and rescue team work day and night. The **control centre** staff answer emergency calls. They send out the firefighters. »

Call handlers at the control centre answer 999 calls.

» Many other staff help to run the fire and rescue service. For example, there are teams that design and buy the **equipment**. Others tell people how to prevent fires. »

>> The firefighters go to emergencies on fire engines. They put out fires and save people from danger.

A fire and rescue team outside their fire station. The man who is not in uniform runs the office.

The fire station

Most firefighters work two days and two nights each week. During their **shift**, they work at the fire station. They check all the equipment, including the fire engines, and do training. »

The fire engines are kept in bays at the front of the fire station.

>> The office is called the watch room. The **station administrator** checks the **rota** for the day so he can tell the staff what they need to do each day.

>> The firefighters keep their kit in the **muster bay**. When they go on duty, they put their kit by the fire engine, ready to put on quickly.

The firefighters' jackets, trousers and boots are kept in the muster bay.

The fire engine

A fire engine is a truck with many special features. »

metal ladder

back seats for firefighters

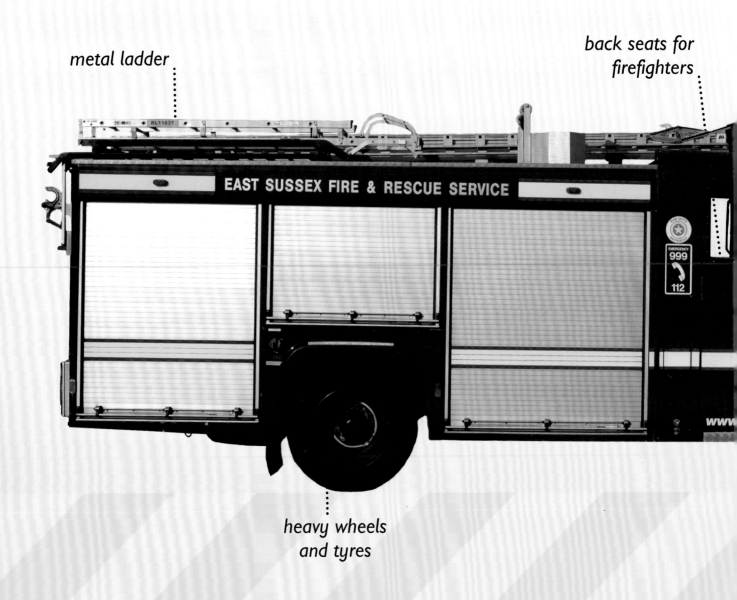

EAST SUSSEX FIRE & RESCUE SERVICE

EMERGENCY
999
112

heavy wheels
and tyres

>> The metal ladder on the fire engine helps firefighters to reach high places. >>

siren *and blue light for warning people to keep out of the way*

······ *driver's cab*

Trainee firefighters pull out the metal ladders to practise reaching people in high buildings.

>> The fire engine has a **hydraulic platform**. It can be raised to allow firefighters to guide people to safety.

This platform lets firefighters reach high places safely.

11

Firefighting equipment

The sides and back of the fire engine open up. All of the equipment is inside.

Firefighters use the equipment to put out fires and to reach people who are trapped. They have axes and **crowbars** to break through windows and doors. A glass saw cuts open windscreens. »

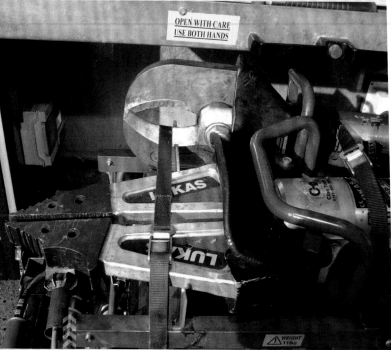

At car crashes, firefighters use these huge cutters to cut through cars to free people.

All fire engines carry a first aid kit and an **oxygen kit** to help people who cannot breathe well. The two green bags are the first aid kit and the oxygen kit. The red and white bag contains instructions for what to do during the emergency.

FIRE & RESCUE SERVICE

E SERVICE

Water is stored in the back of the fire engine. The hoses spray water to put out a fire.

The firefighters' kit

When there is an emergency call, the firefighters quickly put on their uniform over their clothes. »

fireproof **flash hood** protects the head

fireproof jacket ....

hard helmet with **visor** protects the head ....

torch for use in dark buildings ....

thick fireproof gloves

fireproof trousers have **reflective** strips to be easily seen

boots are strong and waterproof ....

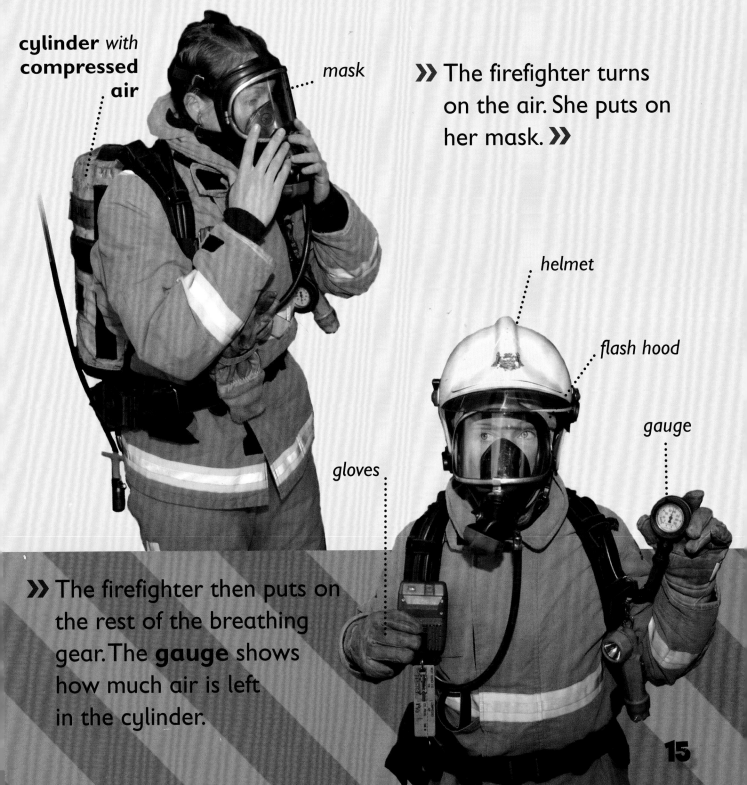

>> **Breathing gear** helps firefighters to breathe where there is lots of smoke or poisonous gas. >>

cylinder *with* **compressed air**

mask

>> The firefighter turns on the air. She puts on her mask. >>

helmet

flash hood

gauge

gloves

>> The firefighter then puts on the rest of the breathing gear. The **gauge** shows how much air is left in the cylinder.

Training to be a firefighter

To be a firefighter, you need to be strong and fit. Trainees find out how to use all the equipment. They learn how to use the powerful hoses and practise using cutting gear. Trainees also learn how to work as a team. »

The trainees roll out the hoses and join them together.

The instructor (right) shows a trainee how to spray water from the hose.

>> Trainee firefighters learn how to save people's lives in an emergency.

In a fire, people may breathe in smoke. It stops them breathing properly. The firefighters learn **resuscitation** – helping a person to breathe again.

The firefighters practise resuscitation using a dummy.

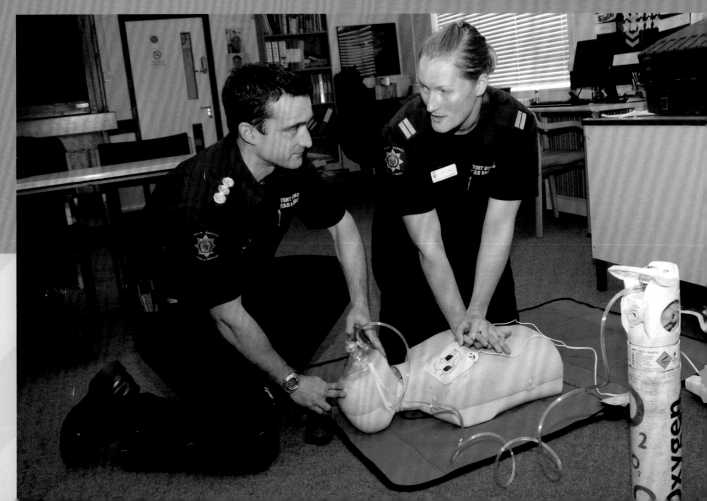

Fire!

If a fire breaks out indoors, you need to get out as quickly as possible. Before you open a door, check if it is warm. If it is, do not open it. Fire may be on the other side. Put bedding or cushions around the bottom of the door to stop smoke coming in. Open the window and shout 'Fire'. 》

Putting cushions around the bottom of a door blocks smoke from coming in.

>> If the door is cool, leave the room.
If there is smoke, stay low down.
The air is clearer near the ground.
Cover your face with a damp towel
or piece of clothing. >>

These young people practise crawling out of the room in case there is a fire.

>> Once you are outside, you should find
a phone and dial 999. Ask for the fire
service. Give your name, phone
number and address.

Fire engines go!

When someone makes an emergency call, the call handler at the control centre rings a fire station close to the fire.

The firefighters hurry to the fire engine. Some fire stations have a pole. The firefighters slide down it to reach the engine bay quickly. »

A firefighter slides down the pole.

>> The firefighters put on their kit as fast as possible.

The firefighters hurry into the fire engine. Five firefighters go out on each engine. They drive safely, but quickly, to the scene of the fire.

The firefighters put on their kit by the fire engine.

The blue flashing light and siren on the fire engine warn road users to keep out of the way.

Rescue

The firefighters reach the fire. Burning buildings are dangerous. The fire is hot, and the thick smoke makes it hard to breathe.

The firefighters put on their breathing gear and rescue any people trapped in the building. Other firefighters put out the fire. »

Firefighters hose the flames of a large fire from a cage held by a crane. They also use the cage to rescue people.

>> Firefighters help in other emergencies, too. After a car crash, they may have to cut away the doors to let people out.

This car caught fire after an accident. Firefighters hose the flames.

>> During **floods**, firefighters rescue people who are trapped in their homes by the water.

Here, firefighters rescue a woman from a flooded road.

Community safety work

Firefighters visit homes, schools and workplaces to check they are fire-safe. They teach people how to make their building safer. They show them what to do if a fire breaks out. Firefighters also hold **open days** at the fire station to tell people about their work. »

A firefighter carries out a fire safety check on a building.

>> Firefighters advise people to fit **smoke alarms** at home and at work. Smoke alarms make a loud sound when they detect smoke. The sound lets people know that they need to get out safely.

Firefighters also advise people to fit a **carbon monoxide** detector at home.

A firefighter fits a smoke alarm.

A carbon monoxide detector.

Fire safety

Follow this simple advice to stay safe at home.

- Never play with matches, candles or fireworks.

- Do not leave toys or clothes on a heater or near a fire.

- Make sure your home has working smoke alarms.

- Plan an escape route so that you can get out quickly. »

This family has made a fire escape plan.
They talk about keeping the doors clear
so that they can get out in an emergency.

>> If a fire does start, you need to get out of the building quickly. Remember to crawl on the floor if there is smoke and check whether doors are warm before you open them (see page 18–19). If your clothes catch fire, you can 'stop, drop and roll' to put out the flames.

A mother shows her daughter how to roll in a coat to put out flames.

Glossary

breathing gear
A kit with a container of air for the firefighter to breathe.

call handler
A person who answers the phone.

carbon monoxide
A dangerous gas that you cannot smell. It can kill people.

compressed air
Air that has been squeezed into a small space.

control centre
A place where emergency calls are answered.

crowbar
A heavy metal bar with a flat end to use as a lever.

cylinder
A container.

equipment
The tools, machines, clothes or other things that are needed for a job.

flash hood
A head covering to protect the firefighter's head from smoke.

floods
When rain or river water covers the ground and does not flow away.

gauge
A device that measures how much of something there is.

hydraulic platform
A platform that is raised using the power of water.

muster bay
The room in the fire station where firefighters keep their kit.

open day
A day when people can visit the fire station and find out what firefighters do.

oxygen
A gas in the air that people need to breathe.

oxygen kit
Equipment containing oxygen that helps people who are having trouble breathing.

reflective
Able to reflect light so it is easy to see.

resuscitation
Helping a person to breathe again.

rota
The list of who is working and when.

shift
The time that a person works, for example, from 7 p.m. to 7 a.m.

siren
A device that makes a loud warning sound.

smoke alarm
An alarm that makes a loud sound to warn people when there is smoke.

station administrator
The person who runs the fire station office.

visor
The front part of a helmet that protects the eyes and face.

Finding out more

Books

Firefighters by Katie Daynes (Usborne Publishing Ltd, 2007)

The Fire Station by Sue Barraclough (Franklin Watts, 2009)

People Who Help Us: Firefighters by Clare Oliver (Franklin Watts, 2006)

Websites

Fire safety for children
http://kids.direct.gov.uk/main.aspx?firstObject=fire_station
Fire safety in the home, with an animation.

Avon Fire and Rescue
www.avonfire.gov.uk/Avon/Kidszone/Kidszone+games.htm
Firework safety, games and quizzes about fire safety

Tyne and Wear Fire and Rescue Service
www.twfire.gov.uk/firesafety/kids/kidsbook/
Downloadable kids' fire safety booklet

Fire safety advice from the Children's Burns Trust
www.welephant.co.uk
Stories, games, quizzes and fire safety information.

Note to parents and teachers: every effort has been made by the Publishers to ensure that these websites are suitable for children, that they are of the highest educational value, and that they contain no inappropriate or offensive material. However, because of the nature of the Internet, it is impossible to guarantee that the contents of these sites will not be altered. We strongly advise that Internet access is supervised by a responsible adult.

Index